D1570965

SAINT JOE'S
PASSION

The Etruscan Press translation and publication of the present edition of *Saint Joe's Passion* has been made possible by a grant from the National Endowment for the Arts.

NATIONAL
ENDOWMENT
FOR THE ARTS
A great nation
deserves great art.

Etruscan Press is a 501(c)(3) nonprofit organization.
Contributions to are tax deductible as allowed under applicable law.
For more information, a perspectus, or to order one of our titles,
contact us at etruscanpress@gmail.com

SAINT JOE'S PASSION

poems by
J. D. SCHRAFFENBERGER

etruscan press

Etruscan Press
Wilkes University
84 West South Street
Wilkes-Barre, PA 18702

www.etruscanpress.org

Publisher's Cataloging-in-Publication
(Provided by Quality Books, Inc.)

Schraffenberger, J. D.
    Saint Joe's passion : poems / by J.D.
    Schraffenberger. -- 1st ed.
    p. cm.
    Poems.
    ISBN-13: 978-0-9797450-3-4
    ISBN-10: 0-9797450-3-9

    I. Title.

    PS3619.C4615S25 2008   811'.6
                    QBI08-600211

Designed by Nicole DePolo

Etruscan Press is committed to sustainability and environmental stewardship. We elected to print this title through Bookmobile on FSC certified paper that contains 30% post-consumer fiber manufactured using biogas energy 100% wind power.

TABLE OF CONTENTS

ACKNOWLEDGEMENTS

"Saint Joe Considers the Furnace," "Saint Joe Considers Smallness of Heart," and "Saint Joe Considers the Foothpath" appear in slightly different form in *the Seattle Review.*

"Invitation to Dinner" appears in *Wild Goose Poetry Review.*

"Saint Joe Considers the Art of Dialing," "Saint Joe's Bar Sinister," and "Saint Joe Considers the Horizon on His Daily Walk" appear in slightly different form in *Syntax.*

Quotations from Catallus are from *The Poems of Catullus* by Charles Martin, and are used by permission of the author.

Shivering with sweat, cold
Tremors over the skin,
I turn the color of dead grass,
And I'm an inch from dying.

—Sappho

For Adrianne

DEDICATION

after Catullus' Poem 1
"I hand this slim book over,
such as it is—for the sake of its patron
may it survive a century or better..."

To the dieback elms and derelict dogwoods
lining my daily walk; to the plastic cheesefood
wrapper whipping in the lunchtime wind;
to cans corroded white; to stubbed gutter butts;
to the drag-footed Japanese teen next door
poking for bottles through neighborhood bins;
to dogwalker standersby waiting for Rover's poop—
you incidentals and sentimentals of life's unlighted labors—
to all of you, and the avenue's corner mailbox
flaking rust chips painted blue into the grass,
I drop this book of newly jetted ink inside
and wait with worn-down stillness for the post.
I give my bunch of trifles unmused. Let it last
no longer than life, copyright lapsed, out-of-print.

SMOKIN JOE

Joseph Johnstone lived his life in takes.
Let's scratch the intro, Joe. Just pick it up at
'because nobody works harder to save you money.'
Erstwhile voice-talent grown humbler,
quiet, *I grow old, I grow older—watch my cherry*
smolder. His trademark pipe melted down
his rotten teeth, ground his voice to gravel,
and then to dust—O smile for us Smokin Joe.
You know who'd be really great for the Flanigan ad?
Who? Smokin Joe. Too bad about him. Yeah,
too bad. All his pipes (Meerschaum, Mahogany,
Briar) forever snuffed now in a rusted sugar tin
his daughter stashed in the garage inside
a lonely moldy box of tinseled holiday garland.

INTO THE NIGHT

Old man Joe believed that life should be
cut off in the sound and living part,
according to the surgeon's rule in amputations,
and if he could be neither sound nor living,
in the truest sense, he was, then, already
too late and should forthwith pack it in—
thus his desperate seizing on that second lucky
life, no longer lived in takes but in the long
lovely moment. *You're listening to…Music…*
*Into the Night…*But O ho ho…*I'm your host…*
Those in the know know…*Joseph Johnstone…*
Behold the old-man spittle on the microphone…
That of course…was J. S. Bach's…Saint Matthew Passion…
the beastly hook of his nose…*Coming up next…*

CANCER

Before he went under, the red-haired nurse
      told Joseph everything would be fine,
            winked the wink of the habitually chummy,
      the ironic wink of gum-chewers
and shoulder-slappers, meant to be lighthearted
      and no doubt kind, but those able to say
            everything will be fine are never those for whom
      everything being fine matters at all.
            Smokin Joe's got a frog in his throat, lumpy
      as a loaf of challah, *Get him a glass*
of water and take it from the top. Cue the vibes.

School Days

Ah, Mr. Joe, Paternostering
your school days away (Our
father who art in college,
Joey be thy name, write
a song, thy voice be dumb,
in class as it is in your dorm room.)

Ah, Mr. Joe, brainy Little Man
on Campus, tutoring all the greeny
undergrads in elementary Physics—
opposite and equal—in Latin—
amo amas amating your way
into their girly earnest lives.

Gail's college hips were narrow
as a boy's, her voice airy
and barely used at all, coming
to you like wind on an otherwise
breezeless day—but you take
what you can get, when offered.

Ah, Mr. Joe, locking sophomore arms
with the chaste and slender Gail.
The co-ed hayride bonfire
smoked your sweater with whiffs
of bologna-spice and ham. Yes, love,

Dear Miss, won't you come to dine
with me, next Sunday after Mass?

INVITATION TO DINNER

after Catullus' Poem 13
"You will dine well with me, my dear Fabullus,
in a few days or so, the gods permitting."

I can only offer up a cool Chanel spritz,
a drop perhaps of vetiver or myrrh,
but I promise, when you come to dine
you will be sated with orris, neroli,
tuberose and pine, a touch of musked
vanilla, the zest of orange and lime.
This is what we've come to, when all
our belly-needs are met, when love
comes pulling up a chair, and table-
cracks ooze with frankincense gum.
The world becomes a wrist to sniff,
clavicle eglantine, sweetbriar broom.
Seconds please for my lingering love.
Suckle this—unguent earlobe, all whiff.

COMING DOWN THE HILL

after Catullus' Poem 1b
"I'd be as pleased with that as Atalanta
was, in the story, with the golden apple
that freed her of virginity's restrictions."

It's like when

    Jack fell down,

  broke his word

and drowned it

  in a pail

    of putrid water,

  and Jill raced

home, told

  her dear Mom

    that Jack's the one

  who loosed

those little pink hips

  from a pair

    of too tight slacks.

Saint Joe Considers the Common Rules of Analysis

*"The first rule was that I would not accept anything as true
which I did not clearly know to be true."*
                                        —Descartes

While you are sleeping deep, dearheart,
            I am tracing the slippery contours
of your body with my littlest eye,
chasing down the source of a soul
            in love. Here is the loosing of pink hips
                        from pressed khaki slacks, and I am Jack,
            a calculus napping inside you, our future
little curly-haired Celeste. This function,
            that function undressed, your black
                        cotton bra so green in sleepless light that
            no more than a glimpse under flannel sheets
do I need to seduce me. There is always
            a moment of similarity that goes with us
                        into darkness, the following of things as whole.

Perhaps we shall lie at length
      and find each hour of the day
  by the hard shadows resolving
on your hips, bright as they are
  in their skin. But perhaps we've
      fallen already, and time is paused
  all around us, passing over each
loveless object—Coke bottle, two
  cups, these hands. So turn over
      here, where sun-white sheets
  are whipping on their clothesline.
Is it too loud to hear a dark voice
  asking Now? and Now? as the light
      settles on the grass next door.

SAINT JOE CONSIDERS THE HORIZON ON HIS DAILY WALK

Note the noise of bouncing balls across the street,
train signals far from here, city buses fading uphill
on Helen Street—the stop that launched a thousand
commutes. Note the upturned trash cans peculiar
to this neighborhood, defined by hobos, by vandals,
by want of sameness, and by differentia, by standing
before the rushing of the lowly Susquehanna. Note
this horizon, its far-off depth closing round about me.

Like a childish huffy Henry, I am shameful, a derision
to all my people, my own name, and all the bright eyes
in America, and all their dying heartfelt keens, could not
have made this love peaceful. But still, you must believe
it is peculiar. You must trust in variance and blindness.
You must trust that want of likeness may someday heal us.

As one preoccupied with the sound and living tissue
of life, Joseph Johnstone, even as a child, fantasized
his own ceremonial execution. O Little Joe manning
right field, crouched like a quiet thoughtful monkey
in the grass, sniffing at his own sweat, the vinaigrette
whiff in the guts of his leather mitt. There General
Johnstone stood before a firing squad. A cigarette?
There Josef the Great puffed his pecs on a gallows.
And there, too, as a ball rolled by the monkey-boy
toward the red-clay warning track, lay the elderly
Man of Letters, Sir Joseph Johnstone in a deathbed,
a breezy canopied affair, yes, diaphanous with white
taffeta sheers, around which gathered all his lovely
progeny, children—men and women with children
of their own, their faces flat and frozen as photos.

A bow-tied grandchild in knickers kneels beside
      the deathbed, his long fingernails trimmed, clean,
   the skin of his small palm soft and warm on the back
of Joseph's cold brown hand. The boy doesn't ask,
     but he's asking with his touch, with his little mousetrap
      eyes, for Joseph's last words. None come, of course.
   Only gnats knabble at his inner ear. True words tote
life around inside them, this much he knows—fragile
     little buckets of life dust. The palm of his mitt is branded
      with big black words: All ★ Star. Something about the stars
    always gives the impression of finality. And yes, the *All*
so perfect, the sky itself inevitable. Joseph the Good
    trips over his cleats. Joseph the Good skips home,
      phrasy with the dust of stars in his pocket.

GRAVITY

On a lurching 727 everybody thought was going down,
Joseph discovered what his most honest last words would be.
Flying always turned him giddy: country turning into town
and city, green hillsides backing finally down, giving way

to cul-de-sacs, fractalesque in their lovely suburban spirals.
Watching from a distance made him very catholic, forgiving
of the world's wide trespasses against him. What were those
trespasses? Even Joseph, perhaps, could not articulate them.

(*But if I could, O such passion!*) He offered help to the elderly,
praised the flight attendants' panache, suffered the chatty,
the driveling kibitz of the middling mobile masses, but always,
eventually, lustily, he fell to savorous empty contemplation,

scarcely noting the erratic bob of a wing, the whir and groan
of engines rousing themselves for flight, the improbability
of tons and tons of metal and flesh defying that most elementary
of physical laws, the one that forever wants to bring us down.

Amore

After the plane righted itself
and people's panting slowed,
tears dried, hearts checked,
the chummy-ironic gum-chewer
next to Joseph straightened
his tie—a graphic designer
from Detroit: *No offense buddy,*
but I don't love you. Then he
laughed and slapped Joseph
three times hard on the chest
(*None taken*) just like a best friend.

Amore Redux

When he tells the red-haired nurse he
loves her (her head a beauteous holy-
    strawberry halo, his own last fat-tongue
        words *love you* like an echo now) she says
    All righty then. She's the daft been-there-
done-that queen of cheery flippancy.
    She gives you the emotional bum's rush.
        She denies you, denies your life, your soul,
    all that might be good and true and right
in the world if only people would listen.
    Sentiment shunted, a wave of the hand,
        O-so-sure-of-herself TV catchphrases:
    I love you. *Isn't that special.* I love you.
Talk to the hand. I love you. *What*-ever.
    And then the nurse pushes the mask
        down harder on his face than she has to.

TEARS FOR A LOST LOVE'S HERRING

after Catullus' Poem 2

"Sparrow, you darling pet of my beloved,
which she caresses, presses to her body…"

O Sparling, my lost love's supper,
whom she's kippered, salt-and-peppered,
whom she stabs her stingy fork through,
you slide your smoked sides inside her,
the most marvelous piece of luck of all.
Ah-ha, so my heart is newly pilched,
desire shining like your split-silver skin.
I suppose the woe and lust that is
in supper will wane, and my hunger pains
might soon be sated: but would that I
could be pickled like you, a slice of lime
beside me, hors d'ouevre and dear.

DEATH OF A LOVER'S HERRING

after Catullus' Poem 3
"O hideous deed! O poor little sparrow!
It's your great fault that my lady goes weeping,
reddening, ruining her eyes from sorrow."

Come O craver of fish, O Saint Joe,
      courter of lost love, bumbler of many hearts.
My old cold lover cooking lunch dredges
a filet through mustard powder for a
      six-minute dip in the toaster-oven broiler.
          Let potatoes on the stove froth and boil over.
Let my lover's hair wrap round her neck
and stick with sweat to her cheek. Come sit
      now to plates garnished with banana leaves
          and lime. No Sir Bones here to complain,
      loudly or no, there ought to be a law.
So let her eyes be steamed-up red
      and swollen, luring me down for this meal,
          serving up my own kippered gullet.

The furnace flares up, abrupt, a smell in the room
      like burnt dust, or smoked meat, an old sweater worn
   for a hayride bonfire and hung far back in the closet.
In warmth, troubling things turn sweet, the mind seizes
      on a fugue—worries get cute, mingle, flirt with the tune.
        Hello, Bach. Fine thanks. I've heard so much about you.
   What disappears will return and pain me later.
It's a simple habit, turning up the heat to 75.
      But in warmth, sweet sad things hatch in my breast.
      This says as much about me as any confession ever will,
      a house heated beyond comfort, *St. Matthew Passion,*
vague memories of the outdoors. When she is asleep
      and I turn up the heat, I think about the moist still
        dreams of warm places breeding behind her eyes.

SAINT JOE CONSIDERS SMALLNESS OF HEART

What pains me will disappear—

     troubled love. I comfort myself

         with words like these:

    no smallness of heart

        can defeat it,

    no sunsteam illness

        in the lungs slow it down,

    no sea-bent Jason

        convince it to behave.

    Never again

shall we put down our sadness

     now that we have

        loved each other so well.

SAINT JOE CONSIDERS THE FOOTPATH

Not even this poem will keep us in good form.
　　Listen. Sleep comes running,
　　　　the rain slips

　　　　down around
　　the trunks of sugar maples
into the creek,

and already we are kept
　　from ourselves.
　　　　No one can stand us.

　　Let's follow the footpath
　　　　home, hang ourselves
　　　　　　to dry.

PASSION

Young Celeste, aimless Celeste, underemployed
fruit of my loins, how ever has a daughter of mine
become so hopelessly hoi polloi? *I've brought you
some Beethoven, Pops.* Though Bach would be better

by far. *That way, when you wake from surgery, Ode to Joy
will be ringing in your ears.* Twitchy Joe fingers the wart
in the crevice between his nostril and cheek.
It appeared overnight at 50, shortly after parting

from his wife for good. He ripped the wart off his face
once in an obsessive late-night fit of cleanliness
before the bathroom mirror, but by 52 it appeared
again with renewed vigor, and now it's like an old

friend, like his pipe had been, ah, like Bach has always
been and ever would be. Celeste presses play,
conducts pianissimo, air-baton out of time,
D minor, yes, *Saint Matthew Passion* would be better by far.

BFF

Mom said to say good luck.

Dozy Joe's swollen throat
hurts like campfire coals, as it has for months—
an ache that became a throb, a throb that became
a quab that became a knob that *voila!*

became the cancer.

Meet your new best friend, Joey.

On the wide
faux-marble windowsill a dried-up fern in its
terra-cotta-like pot presides over the dialogue,
speckles the floor with dead yellow leaves.

*She actually
said to send her best or regards or something like that.*

The cancer that became…

I'm not afraid, you know,
of any of this at all.

Celeste picks up the remote
control, and when the television tingles to life—
Do you mind?—

Josef the Foul snorts, sighs, takes
a grudging interest in the Showcase Showdown
before summoning a nurse with his bedside buzzer.

RECEPTION

This reception sucks and everybody's green.
    (I've seen my spleen and it is green,
        ha ha, my humor's in good humor,
    the tumor, I hear, nothing but a rumor.)
The nurse pokes her little head in the door:
    Whatcha need, Mr. Johnson.
        Celeste changes the channel: *John-STONE.*
    The nurse purses her unpainted lips,
and Joseph the Humble tries on a smile.
    (Whatcha need, O whatcha need, indeed.)
        Miss…? *Arlene. Call me Arlene.*
    Young Celeste chimes in again:
Arlene. Like the hurricane.
    Tropical storm, honey. But I can turn
        any minute now. (Whatcha need,
    O Miss Arlene…I've seen the enemy
and it is pus.) A radio if you please—
    the television is more vexing than relaxing.
        Jesus, Pops. You always sound so…rehearsed.
    (Whatcha need, he he, whatcha need, ho ho…
my words and bones hearsed and re-hearsed.)
    Arlene says *I'll see what I can scrape together.*

PROTECTION

On the screen, a commercial
         for bug spray. Polo-shirted man
    smacking his forearm and neck.
Close-up of disease-carrying mosquito.
      West-Nile. Children playing by creek.
         Woman wielding plastic spray-bottle.
    O Come All Ye Faithful. Behold
the Elixir of Life, my children.
    Celeste turns the volume up, looks back
         at Joseph and points over her shoulder
    at the green-peopled monitor.
Listen, it's one of your old spots. A giggle,
      a titter, a mouthing of the words:
         Because protection is not just a convenience anymore.

How Many at Last?

after Catullus' Poem 7
"My Lesbia, you ask how many kisses
would be enough to satisfy, to sate me!"

One of death at the garden gate, as Judas
gave discreet on the cheek at Gethsemane.

And one of life, unreturned, as upon the cold
rubber-doll lips of the coy Resusci Annie.

And one, if you will, for the wild heart's ease,
twice more in the post-op ring before I rise.

And again as many as the grains of white
Chihuahuan sand, agave scrub, the alluvial

evergreen fan. As many as the tarbush bloom,
the yucca, the whitethorn and tall desert spoon.

Out here, cracking desert crust with our toes,
we are waiting for a lost love's return.

We gawk, we gape, silent and duned, but too few
stars gaze down at these common human desires.

We are mad, unloved dummies, opened up to the sky,
uncounted by what will save us, two lips, a tongue.

Rival

after Catullus' Poem 21

"So give it up now, save your reputation,
or watch out for a savage fucking over!"

Go ahead, sir, hanker forth for my lost
love, Little Miss Schill in your heart-swindling
racket. You're the dirty uncle of appetite,
you're Brother Scam, you're passion's kissing
cousin—all yearn. I can teach the rapacious,
but you remain steadfast, unwild in your craving
and your calculated con. So come here, I've a hand
to play with you, O greed-whore, snake-oiler,
love-monger extraordinaire: stand so I can see
more clearly now what hunger is in your eyes.

Siesta @ Noon

after Catullus' Poem 32
"Honestly, if you want it, give the order:
I've eaten, and I'm sated, supinated!
My prick is poking through my cloak and tunic."

In this, the highest hour, the hottest part
of the day, invite me inside your cool pages
for siesta & uncrook me. I'm curved and
twisted as the ampersand, a bent-low omega
touching his little knobby tilde toes.
I'm burning a hole in the bowl of my poor
lowercase P, so let me come in, stroke me,
loop round me tight as an @ and daub
my sweaty serif with cold Italic cloth.
You'll sprinkle me with ashes, I'll poke you
full of thorns. We'll write this poem together
and bracket our bodies inside. Let's edit out
the wingdings, dear, and trademark our loving:
pink as a newborn, swaddled in Romantic glyphs.

SAINT JOE IN PRAESENTIA

In our house I count seven chairs and one stool.
That way we get two—you plus me. We have
something to parse here, but even I, perhaps,
cannot articulate it. I've made it null anyway.
But you and he, will eventually equal…one?
I consult hypnos, thanatos, brothers to the end,
I'm thinking now of the unspent ripeness
of our love lost: each of us will someday
take the edge or arm of the overstuffed chair,
or choose a quieter place on the floor, and going
back into memory, the blanket glowing somehow
green by the moon, we sit there, still, the scene
moving ready-made through walls into childhood
bedrooms, a sofa full of books, the television blue.

SAINT JOE'S BAR SINISTER

How shall we know in the end
where to stand? These bastard
suburban grasses! The uneven lawn!
In the sinkholes, where the garage
and fence meet, live the rodents
of my heart. So now that you
have reached down with unwrought
hands, down into the wax of a dark
and bloody ground, gone rough now
and desperate, now that we've
been scattered with heat and deep-sea air,
been buried in a bath of sand,
now that the space between us
is a division by naught, how might
anything be known for sure? I'm looking
for a common place, a call for prayer,
a place to love, a deep rodent nest to sleep.

Saint Joe Asks Pardon

"The beauty of Israel is slain upon thy high places:
how are the mighty fallen!"
— *2 Samuel 1:19*

Let there be dew in this absent state
        of waking when the sun elbows through
    hospital blinds. I long for sleep once
more, anoint myself with weariness.
    Too many nights I find by the rising
        and falling of memory to what degree
    the wind has been exhausted. Unexpected
coughs undo my dreamings. I'm done
    reliving the night, I've been through
        the turnstile, I've been shown the sun,
    and calling out undestroyed I will
tell it in Gath. Lost and mean, I will
    publish it in the streets of Askelon. Let
        the daughter of my Philistine heart rejoice.

Voyeur

Suburban schoolboy, Cold-War Cadet, Joey
        uttered only the utterable, the knowable,
    offered up his little life for great and worthy
experiments in personal silence—he woke,
        stretched, looked around his world (the window
            looking into the Helgesons' bedroom, kitchen,
    and living room next door) and vowed to keep
all the unutterable and unknowable things he thought
        to himself: Mr. Helgeson's mysterious penchant
            for standing on his head in the mornings,
        Mrs. Helgeson's fixing of her rubber breasts
in the mirror, a lunch of kippered herring
        and lime: the daily neighborly window display
            he doodled on in his memory all day long.

Silence

Joseph's silence was a pact, an oath
sacred as stars. Some days he failed,
but mostly he did not. Later, the irony
would occur to him that such a man
as he, prone to solemn bouts of quiet,
should make his living with his voice.
O but the words he spoke into those
carefully padded, braced, and boomed
mics over the years were not the pockets
of stardust that made life meaningful.
They were ciphers, meant to mean
little, but hmmm, they *did* so much.

Voice Talent

How many melancholy men, how many winsome wives,
how many loud and careless children had his voice made
    desirous, inconsolable, wanting?

Joseph was—had been, still is on certain channels
at certain times of the day—the rabble's steady beat
    from the bass clef.

A voice-talent, it is said, should have the kind of personality
that just…disappears. Those in the know know how comforting
    disappearance can be.

A voice in the many, another fine-cut suit in a million, the throng,
the madding crowd. By most measures, Old Pro Joe had become
    the loneliest man in the world,

surrounded by people wanting nothing more, or less, than to hear
his voice and never hear him speak. Then his gravel turned jagged
    and tenor turned to wheeze.

And it was Bye Bye, Baby Boy.
    We thank you for the time of your life.

Saint Joe Considers the Sprout

So dry in the cheek as to fall off
with handling, parts of me warmer,
soft, rather coarse. Red patches
on my face that resemble a silk of silk
and worsted skin. Love bores into
the young ones, makes us sick and sorely
men. Endings such as this always disappoint—
the stopping-up of pores, my boiling breaths
put together and sliced thin. So dry
is this face of little reflection, light bending
even in death: white elastic, rotten warts.
Having forgotten such things before, now
as I neaten my hospital linens, they ought be burned.

SAINT JOE TRIES TO BE HALF

The fat gray one appears on the bed,
purring all over, new cold paws on my back.
And I barely remember you. Perhaps it was
this morning you told me you had gone,
but sometimes when light hazards in,
and Emma licks or chews the hair
around my ears, love becomes a reputation,
a robe to put on, a certain kind of bread
to toast. But then the understanding dissolves
in my tea, burns and floats like pipesmoke,
who I will be—in grammar but a noun,
or else I become what a thing is called,
a name naming all my other things—
my love, my life—the same.

WOUNDEDNESS

Gail the Stopgap, Gail the Makeshift, she the tourniquet
tied round Joe's wounded heart, she the willingly tied,
and quiet in her own right, not from existential woundedness,
not from experimental necessity, but for lack of anything to say.

Things quite simply did not occur to her as worthy of expression—
Dumb Mum tending to the tulips and roses in June. Come, dearheart,
take a moment's rest. Hers was a moment-savoring Zen-like temper,
his the temper of a once lazy cat, now altogether canine: O Ruff.

SAINT JOE'S SPLIT

Just about when in bed the body whorl
unlocks and we have taken in the slack,
dip the tip of your finger and cool
my tongue and lips so that we may speak
about our griefs—the strings and cords
are knotted tight about my throat.
The hairs of estimation are split,
but sadly, we've already gone over it all,
and there, where the idols of Egypt
sleep, lies are fallen to me in pleasant
places: keep every other finger dry.
On these every day will we count.
Send your friends away now,
lock the house, please, and go out.

Saint Joe Considers Tuberculosis

A vase of once-white flowers now dried
and unbearably yellow. The hairs
on my skin prickle. I sit here,
calculating the existence of real blood
flowing through real veins. I sit
at the kitchen table reading from a book
affected with numbers, my legs underneath
rubbing out the route of least resistance,
calculating, spreading myself in all directions
I am able. On my skin the nightsweat
of hectic fever in the spine, setting,
settling in. Those who are free from it,
those who listen every day, will swell and cry,
become dead like flowers and humble.

SAINT JOE'S COUNTERPART

Patterns of shame turn up in my college
notebooks. I read them as new-born poems,
as molds in the sand of memory's backyard
playboxes—some things resemble pieces
of something else, legs pulled apart and open,
easing out from some point, some other bent
of mind numbed but still moving, bending
and tending, still something else—a plumb
line going in, toward the center, taking all
the ends together, like frenzy, the order of it
considered, descending into our weaker parts,
where someone else's lovely poem gets
written by someone else's hand: several lovers
loving each and each other alone and trembling.

MAGNETISM

Joseph suffers conversation and longs
        for sleep: this is the great tragedy of his life.
There are so many other minor tragedies besides.
What some mistake for wisdom or simply shyness
        or sheer stupidity is in fact a deep and lasting
                lack of faith—a bond with his disbelief.
And like magnets coming together, the bond grows
stronger the closer he comes to it. One day,
        not long ago, during the seventh take of a cell phone
                spot, the magnet of his disbelief clicked onto his heart,
        and he walked out of the studio, aware that
someday very soon all of his previous ties would
        unravel. *Maybe he just needs a break. Maybe he needs*
                to be alone. It's unlike Joe to be so...unprofessional.

TAKE ONE

Mom's taking some pottery class at JCC. Celeste takes off
her corduroy jacket, hangs it over the arm of the chair.
The jacket makes a slow slide to the floor. *She comes home
all cheery and stupid. She's all like*—Celeste makes her face
cheery and stupid, waves her hands out in front of her
like a jazz dancer—*like a little girl.* (Someday soon,
someday very soon…the impending loss of fondness
for all the little things we've come to know as life.
Better yet, life itself, hanging like a thin-stringed mobile
over our heads. The slightest breeze, the slightest
breeze.) *I've met someone.* Celeste smiles, like a little girl.
Take one, Joe. Let's get this one right the first time.

CELESTE'S EX

was a rough and tumble hip-hopper,
tangled with the cops, popped Celeste
good once in the gut, once on the schnoz,
drove a pimped-out Toyota slow down
the street, back and forth and back and
called the house every night but hung up
quick, smoked cigarillos on the front porch
till noon, wore his dirty jeans too low and
sold oregeno-dope to putzy neighborhood kids.
On Celeste's left shoulder the eightball tattoo
fades. Old Poppa Joe, let her have another go.

Braggadocio's Delight

after Catullus' Poem 4
"Closer, friends: this little yacht you see before you
says that in her day no ship afloat was swifter."

This mad-yoked tricked-out Corolla, G,
will eighty-six any old moldy ride tonight,
all blaze and blurry and blades like snow-white tines,
and damn if it don't bump like bombs,
rolling up in your Kool-aid and tweetin so sweet
it make my teeth hurt hard, my bone marrow throb.
Look, you can't deny: pin the needle to one twenty-five
and take your chicken-headed shorty for a spin.
Park down by the bay, yo, and beat them skins
till the chains bust out they snare-tight rims.
Listen to that engine whisper its locomotive hiss,
say, *Aluminum, Alloy, Diecast Pump and Grill.*
I lay good hot rubber on highway forty-three.
I sing Toyota sweet to the starlight-winched breeze.

LAST THINGS

One knows one's life has been forsaken
when one must drive oneself to surgery.
Somehow it cheers me as I drive round
the hospital's lot that this may be the last
time I'll have to search for a place to park.
I try remembering all the last things I might
have done today, this week, this month,
this year, et cetera, without realizing they
were last things: last popsicle, last sitcom,
last orgasm. Shouldn't I have savored
them all? the way I am now savoring the last
unbuckling of the safety belt? the last locking
of the car door? the long last walk toward
the automatic doors swooshing great blasts
of air onto the heads of those who enter?

First Things

Summer sun suggests childhood
    and a long list of firsts. First bout
of silence. First existential crisis.
First orgasm. Each falling one
    onto the other. The Helgesons were
        Joey's first smooth-cheeked love:
former Beatniks turned Joneses,
he the husband ever-so-eager-
    to-please, she ever so redolent
        of love. Modest Mary Jones
    putting on her morning cones.
Somewhere in the warped glass
    of Joey's bedroom window there still
        swam the hint of Helgeson love.

SAINT JOE CONSIDERS MUSAK

New father hands
      coming down
through the light
to yank us
      from our big
wet bodies,
our big black
      frown that
comes together
round the chin.

A Minor Tragedy

At 45 wonder-wife Gail found Christ,
turned church, slept with Celeste's
body-builder youth pastor, and of a sudden
resented her station as Joseph the Sullen's
stopgap. *Let him bleed.* When Flabby Joe
found out, he paced with his pipe and then
reasoned himself to sleep. It was not anger
that had set him to pacing. He was simply
trying to discover what he should be feeling.
Cuckoldry was one of Joseph's minor tragedies.
At 47 Gail stashed young Celeste away
at a private school for girls, wandered west
in a Volvo co-piloted by God. Humdrum
hubby chalked one up for the Away Team.

CLIMACTERIC

after Catullus' Poem 51

"To me that man seems like a god in heaven."

Tall tanned rock of a man, my roided-out rival
  Godlike, statuesque in his muscle and bone—
    he brushes up against you in the quad
  with a Schwarzenegger smile.
Young Pastor Bloom, you cake-brained flirt,
  you don't deserve the icing of her notice.
    I'm numb and dumb with doubt
  when I see her glazing over others with a glance,
my fat tongue silenced, puffed-up pecs ache.
    Her voice carries crumbs to me and has its way
      with my gut, eyes now blinded
  with a new sacred rage I can't quite place.
Poor pallid poet, why don't you work out?
  You take your time and pose on paper
    like somebody's gonna look twice.

MIRABILIA: FOR MARY

Blindness
to the world
     and all its
     troublesome pains
will be
your guide
into heaven.

        The ringing
           of goodbyes
        will sound
        like buzzing
        and clicks,

        and sadly
        each of us
        will forget
           the other
        so that
        light will
        be as water,

     and water
     as water.

TRAGEDY

The Helgeson story of Joey Johnstone's
childhood surfaces again and again:
contented thirty-something love
turns tail when man takes his own life,
leaves a young newly-ill wife to waste away
next door. A shame, it was said, a scandal
of the worst kind. One evening, months
after her husband was in the ground
but before cancer stole her beauty whole,
Joe watched the woman through his window
weeping herself into a ball on the bed.
In this moment of severest grief Joey saw
bereft Mary Helgeson, like smoke, like a ghost,
just…disappear. When she uncurled,
he could see through her, and she through him.
One moment of cruel eye-contact.
It was curtains after that.

GOING UNDER

after Catullus' Poem 5
"Lesbia, let us live only for loving."

Let's die together, dear, let's drown,
and all those petty poets telling you to live
will peel away like the paper they're printed on.
Moons may glow, and moons may wane,
but when our deep dark love has gone under,
the day will be as stars bobbling in the sea.
Give me a million yesses, a thousand nods more,
and when we've tallied up our nuzzles,
cuddled inside them like cozies,
in a wink we'll be the wiser,
in water the oceanic sink.

Mirabilia Redux: For Gail

A young
woman,
      my light-haired
      lover,
understandably
earnest
about the
heavens,

points to
what might save us:

           meteoric
           stones
           white
           with heat
           like bone,

           every body's
           skin like
           some pale
           fruit.

WANTED

after Catullus' Poem 25
"Peel my possessions from your gummy fingers & remit them,
lest your smooth fanny & your precious mollycoddled hands
be scribbled upon, covered with rude graffiti by the whip's lash."

My dear Mister Bloom, you taker of little things,
you gluttonous grabber of trinkets and tsatskes:
give me back my heirloom watch, my naked-
lady Zippo, the three I-Ching coins you filched
at dinner last Thursday night. O Mister Bloom,
compulsive thief, I imagine you twirling my old
brass fob, and I lose sleep: on my bedroom walls
now I have pasted a thousand posters of your
wanted face. Two thousand Xerox-black eyes
watch me tossing myself to sleep, my dreams
handled by those crooked fingers of yours,
turned over, stroked like rabbit fur as though
for luck, as though to soothe—and me imagining
how they'll slide so smoothly into your hip pockets.

RADIO

Old Cancer Joe suckles at the teat of Arlene's
scraped-together radio, a pathetic little transistor job
with a duct-taped antenna and a grimy dial face.
In Joseph's imagination a blue-jumpsuited janitor
dances with said radio pressed against his ear.

Celeste has forgotten her thrift-store corduroy,
lying there on the floor gathering dust at the base
of the AC, and her scent—jasmine, lavender,
rose—lingers. It mingles with the sanitary smell
of band-aids, ammonia, the distant hint of vomit.

Radio Redux

NPR convinces Joe to nap. Senatorial soundbites,
presidential pundits, more flooding in the Midwest.
He half-listens with a professional ear to the voices,
the control of breath and sound: the sibilant s,
the poppy p, clumsy clusters of consonants.
Few know it is not these sounds that give
voice-talents fits, but the space between them.
Anyone can train his voice to say certain words
with the utmost aplomb, words like *texts*.
Oh, but try putting these words in the context
of all the silence that surrounds them. These
are voices of journalists, smart to be sure,
with a natural flair for articulation, but so few
have honed their voices: unstudied all:
none are talents proper. Smokin Joe dozes
saying the day's headline phrases over to himself
before sinking into an empty, silent sleep—
Poor planning plagues polling places. Congress
critiques conservative candidate. Terror takes its toll.

SHADOWS

Dvorak wakes Joseph, D flat humming inside
his chest. The *"New World" Symphony*, wet
with nostalgia: his room dark now, humid
with his own breath. Joseph imagines someone,
a shadow body, is lying in the empty bed
next to him, and is that a death rattle or only
the wind? After Dvorak comes Mahler.
Then a new voice. *This is Craig McAllister,*
and you're listening to Music Into the Night.
Then Wagner. Then Ravel. Then the voice
again. Jumpy Jealous Joseph turns the volume
knob down and clicks the radio off: his throat
Craigish, tender with a McAllisteresque throb.

The distant sound of a television four doors down,
a cough, a cry, earmarked pages in half-read books:
we do not wear a garment, my dear Nurse Nothing,
but a disguise. Out of the light of blue mooned skies
behind the blinds, seeking by reference to the stars,
for what...? We fumble, garish with this painted face,
slavish as we are in the clown's big red feet, his nose,
his wig and smile and eyes like ice: we remain silent
in this place among the medical facts, among so many
unwritten, unread pages: the ugly growth in my throat
is lost love welcomed home, marks on a paper that is
flesh on my brittle old bones, a book of sounds held,
a forever-long gesture of dying paused all around us:
this pronunciation of lies—I admit no other order but
my own, clavicle yawning round the meaning of bone.

Saint Joe's Wager of Battel

If you came to me once more
in the cold outside and said nothing,
if the subject of our being together
became naive, childish, if these trains
scraping through the city or these next-door
voices went silent and dead—content
with the mere hum of light all the same—
even we rude people of the world
would get it, and nothing would unsettle
the question in my head, circling
around my sleeping self, making
oaths, balming this pain—every night
we fight till the stars shine a little.

Nurse Nobody answers the midnight buzz,
    head and shoulders poked round the door.
Poet Joe wants paper and pen. A few instructions
from the grave. He picks at his wart.
    Maybe he will take it off again tonight.
        One last bloody wound. Hard to see
    Arlene's face in the half-light from the hallway,
but the dark shadows of her eyebrows
    arch up into the center of her forehead.
        Nodding, speaking. *You're going to be okay,*
    you know. Everything will be fine.
Ah, yes, but what does that mean,
    my nursey-pooh? What indeed,
        O corpse-watcher, my funereal muse!

Saint Joe Considers the Spat

1. why we choose *doorknob*,
>   cloak what we mean by closure in,
>   say, love, when we want to burst forth,
>   tear down the drywall.

2. why things *unhinge*.

3. why certain words suggest the door,
>   or the bath, ill-fit shower-rings,
>   steamed-up glass,
>   just the right amount of soap
>   to close up the eyes.

4. why we tend to run,
>   lock ourselves inside,
>   weep into our hands
>   on closed toilet seats,
>   ponder cracked tile,
>   the chipping grout.

5. why lovers love each other
>   so they slip away
>   into the shower,
>   wash what worries them
>   right out of their hair.

TAKE TWO

Adieu, adieu, kind Arlene. Joseph rubs
the ribs of corduroy against his cheek.
Ah, the final rub. In the jacket pocket:
string, grit, a piece of licorice,
a folded receipt. The lamp on the wall
behind his head casts a blue-white halo
onto the bed. The receipt: Hershey's
Chocolate, Tom's of Maine, Sure Sign
EPT: *Take Two, Joe. The prompter's on.*
In the bed next to him, beyond the halo
of light, the bow-tied dreamchild
in knickers, oxygen mask strapped tight,
steamed up white, and the young
Mary Helgeson at his side, patting
the boy's small hand, listening, but not
a peep—Joseph's heart unclicks. Not yet—
the stars inevitable out the window.

In Wait

after Catullus' Poem 52

"Catullus, what keeps you from killing yourself? No good reason."

Why wait, Poor Joe, lingering on the stars?
Your buddy Tommy Tumor really wants to play,
and isn't the daylight over here brighter anyway?
Why pause, Poor Joe, for the paltry little stars?

BOOKS FROM ETRUSCAN PRESS

Legible Heavens | H. L. Hix

A Poetics of Hiroshima | William Heyen

American Fugue | Alexis Stamtais

Drift Ice | Jennifer Atkinson

The Widening | Carol Moldaw

Parallel Lives | Michael Lind

God Bless: A Political/Poetic Discourse | H. L. Hix

Chromatic | H. L. Hix (National Book Award finalist)

The Confessions of Doc Williams & Other Poems | William Heyen

Art into Life | Frederick R. Karl

Shadows of Houses | H. L. Hix

The White Horse: A Colombian Journey | Diane Thiel

Wild and Whirling Words: A Poetic Conversation | H. L. Hix

Shoah Train | William Heyen (National Book Award finalist)

Crow Man | Tom Bailey

As Easy As Lying: Essay s on Poetry | H. L. Hix

Cinder | Bruce Bond

Free Concert: New and Selected Poems | Milton Kessler

September 11, 2001: American Writers Respond | William Heyen

etruscan press
www.etruscanpress.org

Etruscan Press books may be ordered from:

Consortium Book Sales and Distribution
800-283-3572
www.cbsd.com

Small Press Distribution
800-869-7553
www.spdbooks.com